To Sandra and Don,
with memories of our
happy times (together!
Our love,
Stephanie
and
Carla

Ossabaw

A SENSE OF PLACE

MERCER UNIVERSITY PRESS

MACON, GEORGIA | 2016

Island

PHOTOGRAPHS BY JILL STUCKEY

NARRATIVE BY EVAN KUTZLER

FOREWORD BY JIMMY CARTER

MUP/ H926

© 2016 by Mercer University Press
Published by Mercer University Press
1501 Mercer University Drive
Macon, Georgia 31207
All rights reserved

9 8 7 6 5 4 3 2 1

Books published by Mercer University Press are printed
on acid-free paper that meets the requirements of the
American National Standard for Information Sciences—
Permanence of Paper for Printed Library Materials.

ISBN 978-0-88146-603-4
Cataloging-in-Publication Data is available from the Library of Congress

Book design by Burt&Burt
1865 map courtesy Library of Congress

Printed in Canada

Contents

Main Road, looking south

Foreword

I HAVE HAD THE PLEASURE OF VISITING OSSABAW ISLAND MANY TIMES SINCE THE 1970S. During my term as governor of Georgia, Sandy West invited me, Natural Resources director Joe Tanner, and other state officials to visit the island. We saw what a precious resource her family owned and we listened to their dilemma. Increasing property taxes in Chatham County made the family's continued ownership of Ossabaw impossible, so Sandy and her family faced two choices: preserve the island by selling it to the state, or sell it to a private investor for a higher price. Ossabaw is what it is today because Sandy fought to preserve it, enlisted the support of others, and, in the end, made compromises that put the future of the island ahead of self-interest. Working with Sandy, Joe Tanner and I developed a provisional deal in 1972, and six years later, the island became Georgia's first heritage preserve.

Ossabaw Island, A Sense of Place exhibits a collection of Jill Stuckey's photographs of Ossabaw Island. Jill is an expert photographer who is especially adept in capturing the intangible essence of the island. Alongside her views of the wildlife and historic buildings, the photographs and Evan Kutzler's essays offer glimpses into the life and work of Roger Parker, the "Saltwater Cowboy," who has worked on the island since before I left the Navy in 1953, and who, as I have learned from many delicious meals in Plains, is quite a good cook. Funded by my friend Wayne Johnson, who has a longstanding interest in environmental responsibility, the book also discusses efforts to preserve the important natural and cultural resources of the island for future generations.

In sharing these stories through photographs and essays, *Ossabaw Island: A Sense of Place* highlights the many ways people have experienced the island, with great attention given to the visual and nonvisual perceptions of the place. Reading about Ossabaw recalls my own early experiences in nature, especially listening. Long before my daddy let me own or even handle a gun, he let me tag along on fishing trips, follow him as our dogs found elusive quail, and pick up the winter doves he harvested. As I have reminisced in *An Outdoor Journal*, the only sounds that broke the still morning air when the group of hunters met in downtown Plains, Georgia, came from roosters and newly awakened songbirds.

Safe and successful hunting in the early morning hours required careful listening. From the woods came the calls of unseen barred owls, and from the fields came the sounds of killdeer landing and flying off. As morning approached there came the overlapping sounds of crows, songbirds, bobwhite quail, and finally what the hunters were listening for—the whistle of doves' wings over our heads. During these moments we tried not to move or make a sound. In addition to enjoying the silent communing with nature, there are many good reasons to protect the environment, and allowing future generations to have similar experiences in places like Ossabaw is one of them.

Pairing Jill's photographs with Evan's writing tells an important story about a special place. It is an interesting and compelling new look at an old and lovely island. Much like the island itself, this book is worth exploring.

Jimmy Carter
38th President of the United States
Plains, Georgia

Introduction

SOME ISLANDS ARE EASIER REACHED THAN OTHERS. Requiring a boat and permission, Ossabaw is one of the most difficult of Georgia's Golden Isles to reach today. Weather and tides also factor into its accessibility. At low tide the route is longer and more treacherous. Thick fog can leave someone on the mainland or the island for days. When Jill Stuckey and Roger Parker go to Ossabaw, the shortest water route is six miles. This remoteness is part of Ossabaw's appeal. Although Jill has been going to the island for more than two decades, she uses the term "giddy" to describe the feeling each time she is en route from the mainland to Ossabaw Island.

Jill became a local expert in her twenty-two years exploring the island. In 1993, she worked for the Environmental Protection Department with the State of Georgia inspecting fuel tanks. Later she helped initiate the effort to install an underwater power line from Skidaway Island to Ossabaw to save the state money and protect the environment. When sudden cardiac arrest required Jill to receive a pacemaker in 2007 and her husband, Gene, was tragically hit and killed by a truck in early 2008, Ossabaw became a source of comfort and strength. Exploring the island by foot and truck with the company of her Jack Russell Terrier, Tom, Ossabaw put Jill's mind in a better place, and her island adventures led to the photography exhibited in this book.

This project combines Jill's photography with glimpses into the island's human and natural history. All projects require choices, and the scope of this book is both selective and interdisciplinary. It combines art and public history as well as environmental studies and the humanities. At first, this approach led to differing visions about the shape of the final product. Jill modestly thought it would be a history book with photographs. However, we decided that it was a photography book with history—and not the other way around. We also decided to include Jill's conventional photographs alongside her high-dynamic-range work. High-dynamic-range is an old technique that combines photographs of the same scene taken at different exposures with a resulting product somewhere between the realistic and the imaginative. Finally, for ease of viewing and reading, we decided to include only minimal captions and convert footnotes into a short bibliographic essay at the end of the book. Such an evolving conversation is typical for collaborative, interdisciplinary projects of a creative nature.

First and foremost, this book exhibits Jill's photography, but there are multiple ways to use and enjoy the volume. Vignettes throughout the book share insights about the life and work of Roger Parker, Ossabaw's "Saltwater Cowboy," and those close to him. The photographs provide a way to experience the landscapes, the flora, and the fauna of the island from the comforts of the mainland. Short chapters supplement the photography by discussing elements of Ossabaw's environmental history as well as its historic and modern multisensory landscape. In this way, Jill's photographs are the eyes of the book, and the text, when appropriate, brings to the surface the sounds, smells, tastes, and touches that all contribute to the island's power of place. The nonvisual senses—so important to the ordinary and extraordinary aspects of everyday life—are too easily overlooked when one relies on vision alone. That is what makes this book experimental and unique. Although this book can be read from cover to cover, it is not necessary to start at page one or to go in chronological order. Explore the book as you would discover the island.

Bradley Beach

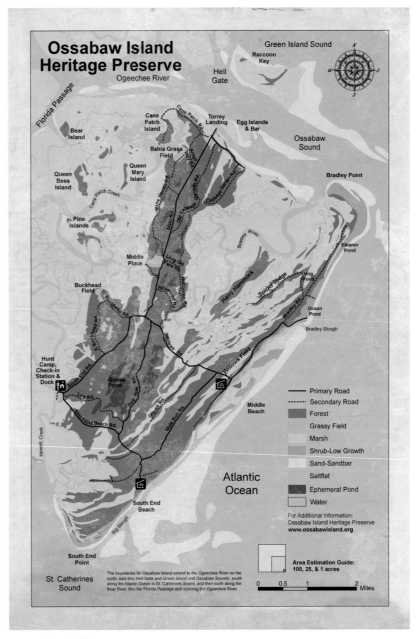

Ossabaw Island, 2010

1

Finding Ossabaw

BY ACCIDENT, ROGER STAYED OVERNIGHT ON OSSABAW ISLAND when he was 16 years old. It was 1951, and the island manager, Mark Sawyer, had purchased ninety-five head of cattle from Roger's uncle, Arthur Graves, and father, Arthur Parker. Roger was cheap labor. Loading up the cattle on a barge, he left Savannah and headed toward the island in the afternoon. Roger knows every inlet and channel around the island today, but on that day his contribution involved following instructions and driving the cattle where they were supposed to go. The barge left for Savannah. Uncle Arthur would see that Roger got back to the mainland.

As the sun set, Roger unloaded the cattle at a landing and separated them into particular fields. Then he returned to the Boarding House where his aunt and uncle lived on the northern edge of Ossabaw's high ground. Although a remote island, the wealthy family who wintered on Ossabaw had installed a telephone line from the mainland. It was on this line that bad news came to Roger's hosts. There was a death in the family. Roger's aunt and uncle took the last boat for the mainland, leaving him on the island by himself. He did not sleep at all that night.

Places, humans, and animals change when the sun sets. There is a certain element of magic at night that enriches the sensory experience of place. Yet this enhancement comes with dangers. Decades later, when Sandy West brainstormed what became the Genesis Project on Ossabaw in 1970, she initially considered bringing at-risk youth to the island. "Total silence and total darkness," she said, "are two things that freak them out the most." Her goal was to utilize the sensory impact of Ossabaw as first an instrument of terror and then an instrument of self-reflection and personal growth. A young rancher in 1951, Roger was at-risk in his own unique way, and there were good reasons to be afraid of the dark. Under an overcast sky, a new moon, and without the proper tools, near-total darkness can feel unwelcome even at places most inviting by day. Night encroaches on personal space and overwhelms the eyes by denying them visual information.

While Sandy was right about darkness, Roger heard more than just silence that first night. The sounds of human activity were greatly diminished. Roger heard no motor vehicles. Trees and waves either absorbed or overpowered human noise from Richmond Hill or Savannah. Absent of human noise, the island also lacked the orderly, bucolic quietude that made the rural Georgia low-country feel tranquil. Erratic, often unidentifiable noises pierced the background sounds of nature.

Fear of these sounds has deep roots in human thought. When early European settlers first arrived on the same coast hundreds of years ago, they expressed ambivalence about the sounds of semi-wild America. Often, settlers turned to the book of Deuteronomy to describe unsettled land as a "howling wilderness." The earliest settlements stayed within earshot of the sea. The howling interior was a land of opportunity, but also danger.

Some of the elements of nature that howled to early settlers called out to Roger in 1951 and continue to resonate in the twenty-first century. Unlike our eyes, our ears are always vigilant. They have nothing comparable to eyelids, so they receive stimuli whether welcome or not. In the wild this can lead to terror as easily as awe. A slight breeze, refreshing on Ossabaw during a summer day, leads to goose bumps at night. From a tree near the marsh comes the sound of an unseen bird. A grunt from a feral hog comes from the bushes. Something steps on a branch and makes a loud cracking sound. Such sounds might go unnoticed during the day. At night they are the building blocks of terror. Plato, Aristotle, and other Western philosophers have considered sight the most rational of the five senses for thousands of years, but unmitigated night renders our eyes senseless. The power of emotion and primordial fear rises as the sun sets. Night undermines assumptions about power in the animal kingdom. Are humans the hunters or the hunted? At night it can be hard to tell.

In 1951, Roger could not have known he would spend most of his life on Ossabaw Island. His tenure on the island has involved a give-and-take relationship with nature. The work was humbling. Many of the fences Roger labored to build in the 1950s and 1960s have all but vanished. Many of the buildings that once teemed with life are now abandoned. People have come and gone. The island has changed in some ways and remained the same in others. Yet through all these changes in the land, Roger has been the constant, the "Saltwater Cowboy."

Gate to Main House

Boats at Torrey Landing

SHAPED LIKE A HEART OR AN ARROWHEAD, Ossabaw Island is ten miles long, eight miles wide, and contains approximately 25,000 acres. The salt marshes take up about 16,000 acres, leaving about 9,000 acres of higher ground that is not influenced by the ebb and flow of tides. Crisscrossing the high ground are dozens of narrow dirt roads, some of which date back hundreds of years.

Near the northern terminus of the island is Torrey Landing, one of the island's many historic landings, named after the industrial family from Michigan who purchased the island in 1924. The extant historic buildings near North End are located within a one-mile radius of the landing. Each provides a tangible link to some part of Ossabaw's past. Down the palm alley from Torrey Landing is the Club House. This prefabricated building came to the island by ship about 1886. The chimney on the eastern elevation of the house, however, predates the rest of the building. The Club House sits on one of at least four plantation sites on the island, at the northern end of Main Road. This chimney is likely the last vestige of those plantation houses built in the eighteenth and nineteenth centuries. The layers of the house's architectural features, like the island itself, are illustrative of the island's layers of history. The chimney is a visual reminder of a nearly invisible past.

Approximately one mile southeast of Torrey Landing is the Main House, an example of an early twentieth-century "country estate" with a red-tile roof and pink stucco walls. Designed by Savannah architect Henrik Wallin and built by Faquar McRae, the building exhibits a subtle Spanish Colonial Revival style that gestures to the island's earliest colonial encounters. The fifteen-bedroom mansion sits amid a minimally landscaped area of shade trees that has replaced an elaborate complex of gardens, designed but not fully implemented by Ellen Biddle Shipman (1870–1950), a female pioneer in landscape architecture. Nationally known for her landscape designs in the early twentieth century, Biddle's work at Ossabaw appeared in *The Garden History of Georgia* in 1933. Although most elements of the gardens, which extended in front and far behind the Main House, are gone, some landscape features remain. Behind the house are two ponds, one named "Peter Pan Pond," with sculptures of Peter Pan and Tinker Bell, and another interesting for its ornamental use of two cement trees that—until touched—are quite deceiving to the eye.

West of the Club House sits the Boarding or "Bachelor's" House, an early twentieth-century Craftsman-style bungalow, adjacent to an early nineteenth-century tabby building referred to as the "Oyster House." The Boarding House began as a duplex for an island superintendent and a hunt master in the decades before the Torrey family purchased Ossabaw. After the Torrey family purchased the island, workers constructing the Main House may have lived here. The nearby Oyster House has a multilayered history. Built as a smokehouse in the early nineteenth century, it later served as a storage unit, as housing for an electric generator, and as a place for oyster roasts.

Saddlebag-style tabby slave quarters—the rarest buildings on the island—are tangible reminders of the island's transnational connections and deep history. Enslaved people built one of the buildings in the 1820s and the other two in the 1840s. After being vacant for decades, they were converted into tenement housing for blacks and whites in the early twentieth century. These buildings exemplify the blend of plantation architecture and international building traditions. Organized as duplexes for efficiency, not comfort, around a central fireplace, each tabby probably served as home for two families during slavery. The tabby construction style, a combination of shells, sand, lime, and water, had a far reach, including the Mediterranean and West Africa. And lastly, the physical shells used came from the midden mounds that abound on the island and date back thousands of years. In 1995, the National Trust for Historic Preservation highlighted these buildings when it listed Ossabaw Island as among the eleven most endangered historic places in the United States.

Club House

Main House

Heading south from Torrey Landing is Main Road, and smaller roads branch off this main artery. Enormous live oaks line both sides of Main Road for miles, representing some of the biggest trees and oldest living things on the island. The alley of live oaks is also one of the island's most significant examples of massive landscape architecture. It is the oldest existing road on the island and one of the oldest preserved dirt roads still in use. Stone mile markers dating to at least the early nineteenth century extend in reverse order southward from North End. The first marker has the number five cut into the stone, indicating that at least four more mile markers stood somewhere south of that point.

Near the island's geographic center is Middle Place, named after the mansion that once stood west of Main Road. High, level, and located near artesian springs, Middle Place's history is measured in millennia. Near Middle Place is one of the largest known prehistoric sites, the location of a succession of Native American villages dating from at least AD 500 to about 1500. The nineteenth-century plantation house at Middle Place remained until the early twentieth century, when it disappeared from the landscape, but according to a surviving map from the 1850s, it was located in the field between Main Road and the marsh. Remnants of the mansion's outbuildings and slave quarters remain. Unlike the tabbies at North End, where continued use by tenants in the twentieth century preserved the tabby structures, only the foundations and fragments of walls remain at Middle Place.

Pausing at Middle Place, there is a feeling of abandonment. For millennia, humans called this place home. Somewhere in this vicinity, a group of African Americans established a community after slavery and lived there until the end of the nineteenth century. Yet the island has erased any clear evidence of their town. Extant buildings at Middle Place represent projects undertaken by the Ossabaw Island Project in the 1960s and '70s. The programs helped lay the groundwork for the establishment of Ossabaw Island as Georgia's first heritage

Main House courtyard

Sunrise at South End Beach

preserve in 1978. Someday, those buildings, too, will be gone. All that will be left are the subterranean foundations, a scatter of tools and trash, and photographs of the site. The island continues to slowly but relentlessly reclaim its land.

Beyond Middle Place, Main Road splits, one branch heading toward South End Hunt Camp and the other taking advantage of the high causeway. Both roads pass through marshes abounding with alligators and birdlife. Bearing to the right (west), South End Beach Road is met by a turnoff for a third historic plantation site at Buckhead Field. Shortly before reaching South End Field, formerly the location of a fourth plantation site, the road passes an unceremonious graveyard for the parts of hogs and deer not removed from the island by hunters. Here, skulls and other bones litter the ground. At this place, it is not uncommon to see vultures and the occasional eagle feasting on the remains of a successful deer or pig hunt. The road then turns to the southeast, passing the largest live oak tree on the island and "Hell Hole Road" on its way to South End Beach.

Bearing to the left (east), the route becomes Willows Road and passes a series of marshes along a causeway heading in the direction of Middle Beach. The landscape changes from the older, higher Pleistocene ridge into a younger, lower, and wetter Holocene plain, with its accompanying marshes and interspersed woods. The narrow road meanders just a few feet above water teeming with alligators and other life. The marshes, along with Rockets Pond and Willows Pond, are among the more remote parts of the island. During warm months, the air is thick with the sounds of birds, insects, and marine life. During the winter the nights are a silent, acoustic desert. The only sounds come from airplanes in the sky, where only satellites and planes, along with the faded lights of distant stars, break the darkness. Near the eastern edge of the island, Mule Run Road extends south, connecting with South End Beach Road near South Beach.

Smaller roads and place names hint at past land uses. Along Willows Road, First and Second Cedar Dump point to the 200-year history of timbering on the island. Log Road on the south side of the island and Pine Barren Road and Pine Barren Pond on the north indicate the prevalence of that industry around the island. Rice Pond and Cabbage Garden Road, both on the north side of the island, indicate past agricultural practices, one for commercial sale and the other for subsistence.

Whether traveling Ossabaw by foot or by car, on roads or through the woods, there are two contrasting qualities of the place. For those steeped in the history of the low-country, there can be, at times, a sense of abandonment. Evidence of the human labor that shaped the island is abundant if one knows what to look for: occasional fence posts, primary tree growth over old fields, and periodic ditches crisscrossing the landscape are reminders of the human energy put into Ossabaw. A contrasting and more compelling quality is the sense of wildness. The roads appear as though they just came into being without the hands of men and women. At dusk, one is likely to see hogs, raccoons, armadillos, and the occasional alligator in the headlights. This enveloping sense of wildness is the subject of the next chapter.

Boarding House

Hell Hole Road

Cane Patch Road

End of the road at South End Beach

Island vulture

Road to South End Beach

2

Sensing Wildness
Ossabaw's Flora and Fauna

"In wildness is the preservation of the world."
Henry David Thoreau

WHAT, PRECISELY, DO WE MEAN WHEN WE USE WORDS like *nature* or *wilderness*? On the word nature, twentieth-century literary critic Raymond Williams commented, "Any full history of the uses of nature would be the history of a large part of human thought." Yet outside certain specialized circles, concepts like nature or wilderness are often self-explanatory. When the terms resist easy definition, it is akin to Supreme Court Justice Potter Stewart's refusal to define obscenity by famously declaring, "I know it when I see it." In a similar way, Ossabaw Island presents human visitors with a palpable expression of its own wildness. Much of this has to do with the power of the island's sensory environment. Margaret Keister, who studied the creative process on Ossabaw, described being struck by the island's "myriad stimulations to the senses; its energizing influence on body, mind, and spirit." Keister found the multisensory experience of fully encountering nature on Ossabaw increased visiting artists' creativity.

The island envelops the senses. A forest canopy of pines, oaks, and Spanish moss, combined with the undergrowth of palm fronds, overwhelms the eyes with shades of green and brown. In such places, even people with good mental compasses can become disoriented and then, suddenly, lost. The background sounds of wind, water, and trees—broken only occasionally by the distant whisper of an airplane—produce a calming quietude. During the Ossabaw Island Project of the 1970s and '80s, immersion in this quietude made for introspection and creative discovery. One participant recalled that she could not hear "a single artificial noise" while working on the island.

Whereas artists and creative experts in the twentieth century pointed to the island's sounds as exemplary, the island's name gestures to a different sensory encounter. Scholars believe that Muskhogean-Hitchiti word *ossabaw* meant the "place of the black drink tea" or "where yaupon holly grows." When crushed and steeped into a hot tea, the yaupon holly tree, or *Ilex vomitoria*, produces a strong stimulant that Native Americans along the southeastern coast used as part of purification rituals. According to James Kilgo, who collected *Ilex vomitoria* from near Cabbage Garden Road, the tea has a "a serious taste, somewhere between strong tea and coffee, a wild oaky taste with a bitter edge." Consumed in large enough quantities, the black drink tea acts as an emetic that induces vomiting.

Kilgo's experimentation with black drink brings up an important question about the limitations of sensing the past. The difficulty of reproducing the chemical taste (and smell) of black drink is relatively easy to overcome. The devil is in the perception. When it comes time to make meaning out of raw sensations, Kilgo must measure the experience by the standards of his own time, place, and culture. What is sweet or bitter depends on the experiences of an individual palate and the range of tastes encouraged by a particular culinary culture. Coffee or tea is a good comparison for the present, but we cannot know with specific-

Raccoon

Oldest live oak tree on Ossabaw

ity the mental or spiritual perceptions of those who named the island for its taste. Those perceptions belong to another time, place, and culture.

The haptic (or felt) experiences on Ossabaw intensify the sense of wildness that comes through the eyes, ears, and palate. Gnats, mosquitoes, chiggers, and ticks all seek a close relationship with human skin. One of the students who lived at Middle Place for weeks during the 1970's and early '80's Genesis Project, recalled, "Within the first three days, the bugs had gotten to us tremendously because [they] affected our ability to sleep. You're swatting bugs all night long and in the dawn they're already all over you." While insects are among the smallest living things on the island visible to the human eye, they are also among the boldest. Unless surprised into defensive action, hogs are generally cowards. They use their ears and snouts to sense danger before they see it. Likewise, a careful pedestrian can avoid snakes and alligators, both of which are eager to keep their distance from human intruders. The power of insects is greater than their individual bite. Although an overstatement, the phrase "being eaten alive" by insects is a throwback to days when disease transmission was not the primary concern. Today, the perception of bites and stings gestures to the real risk that comes with every prick of the skin. West Nile virus and Lyme disease are lotteries one hopes not to win.

The senses of Ossabaw are not individually exceptional. There are other places to see dense undergrowth, to listen to quietude, and to be eaten alive by insects. What makes Ossabaw an exceptional place is the sum of those attributes. It is as though the island has its own agenda: it wants you to think it is untouched wilderness. The foliage, the calmness, and the insects collectively proclaim separation from human history. It is as if the humans who transformed the mainland and other islands have not tread foot in these marshes, fields, and woods. The island offers a convincing *prima facie* argument through sensory phenomena. As Ossabaw presents a sensory illusion of history without humans, the island is also a reminder of nature's resilience.

COMPARED TO A HUMAN LIFESPAN, OSSABAW IS ANCIENT. On a geological timescale, however, the island is a youngster. If the natural history of the earth were condensed into a single twenty-four-hour day, Ossabaw Island would come into being within forty-nine seconds of midnight. Geologists do not completely understand the formation process of barrier islands, but the current theory is that a combination of rising sea levels after the last Ice Age, waves, and currents are responsible for their creation. Most of Ossabaw is older than the average barrier island along the Atlantic Coast. Areas of the island west of Bradley River and Jekyll Creek were formed during the Pleistocene era, somewhere between 30,000 and 40,000 years Before Present (BP). The eastern extremes of the island, including South Point, Pelican Point, and Bradley Point, are much younger. They came into existence during the Holocene era, only 1,000 to 1,500 years BP.

Thirteen miles of undeveloped beaches and sand dunes are the part of the island that experiences the fastest natural change. This transformation is visible—even audible—at South Beach, where the ebb and flow of the tides erode the beach at a rapid pace. The process undercuts pines and sand live oaks, leaving them stripped of bark on the beach like wooden skeletons. During low tide, the beach extends far away from the tree line, and the outgoing current textures the coarse, wet sand with a dimpled pattern. To the north, Middle Beach has expanded substantially in the last half century, putting nearly half a mile between the shore and the Torrey family's former beach house. Along the beaches and dunes are ecological communities of birds and sea life. Migratory shorebirds and seabirds, including pelicans and numerous species of tern and gull, can be found around Bradley Beach, where it is common to see up to 2,000 birds. Loggerhead turtles nest along the coast, and Bradley Beach has one of the greatest

Bottle-nose dolphin

Ghost crab

Loggerhead sea turtle

Royal terns on South End Beach

densities of these turtles in Georgia. Middle Beach and South Beach also have large numbers of birds and sea life. Horseshoe crabs lay eggs near the southern point of South Beach, attracting diverse bird populations.

The marshes provide some of the most striking features of the island in sight, smell, and biological diversity. The flow of rivers and the rise and fall of tides provide the rich, muddy soil on which spartina, or cordgrass, thrives. Cordgrass further enriches the soil in two ways. Its roots stabilize the soil and its decomposition further fertilizes the soil. The life, death, and decomposition cycle of cordgrass slowly elevates the marsh. Ultimately, the cordgrass lifts the marsh above the level of the tides, at which point other plants carry on the process.

The 16,000 acres of tidally influenced marshes and creeks on Ossabaw provide a dense resource for a wide range of marine and terrestrial organisms. Single-celled organisms, oysters, crabs, fish, wading and migratory birds, and raccoons, as well as introduced donkeys and pigs, all draw food from, in, or around the marsh. The shallow, brackish water of estuaries provides small fish with protection from larger fish off the coast. Except on cold winter nights, the marshes are teaming with the sights and sounds of life. There is always something to see or hear.

The high ground on Ossabaw supports a maritime forest with occasional clearings and a number of freshwater ponds. The woods are usually quieter than the marsh. These areas have seen some of the most significant human alterations, visible now in the pattern of foliage and occasional remnants of ditches and fence lines. Today it supports a number of different forest communities, each in various successional stages of regrowth. Pine communities, for example, inhabit areas of the island experiencing the newest regrowth. Forests comprised of a mixture of oaks and pine probably represent a later succession of regrowth. Mixed hardwood communities are found in areas with the fewest historical disturbances.

IN SOUNDS, SMELLS, TASTES, TOUCHES, AND SIGHTS, OSSABAW ISLAND gives visitors the chance to engage with nature in a fundamental way. Although humans have been trying to shape the island to meet their needs for 4,000 years, the island persistently abounds with an enveloping wildness. Conservation of the island has reclaimed it as a place where it is possible to experience a sensory aesthetic of wild places. Nature writers and conservationists have gestured to this aesthetic for generations. Big thinkers from Henry David Thoreau and John Muir to Aldo Leopold and Rachel Carson have described nature through the senses. They wrote at different times and picked up on different sensory signals, but the mode of knowing wildness remained much the same.

A walk through the woods or a marsh on Ossabaw is fuel for the imagination. The feeling is nearly spiritual, providing a sense of meaning and continuity across time and place. And in many places, visitors will feel as though they share a connection with those more articulate, more introspective souls who capture universal truths. When Henry David Thoreau went to Walden Pond in 1845, he spent much of his time describing simple living through the visual and nonvisual senses. Many of these resonate with experiences on Ossabaw today. Thoreau identified the smell of musk-bearing animals, scented flowers, and potent pine boughs. Inhaling morning air felt, smelled, and tasted restorative to his body. "It was invigorating," he wrote, "only to sit here and drink and be bathed in this uncontaminated current." While cutting firewood, he remarked how the resin from the green pine boughs imparted his hands with a fragrance that he could taste while eating his midday bread and butter. Even more important were the things not heard. There were few "domestic sounds"—no farm animals, no machinery, and no neighbors. Thoreau imagined himself the only

Conch shell

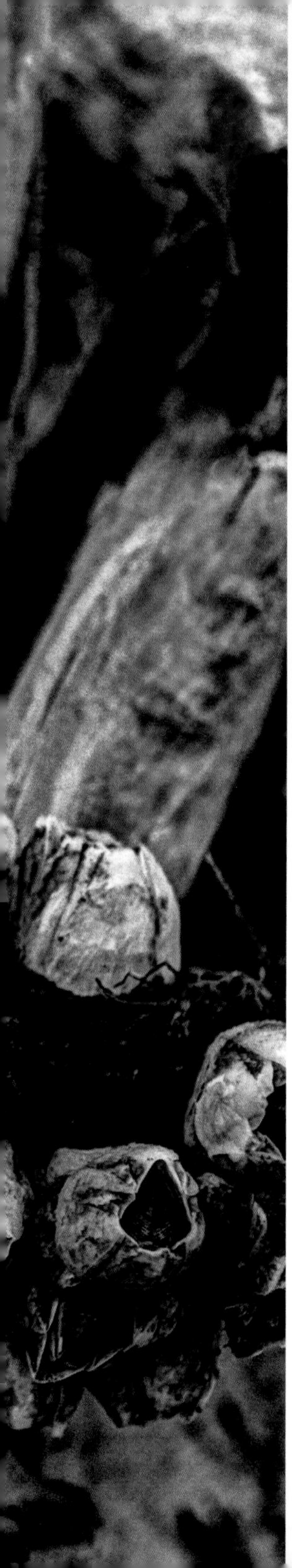

inhabitant in the state of Massachusetts not awoken by the tyrannical morning cry of a rooster.

Although no one would mistake 2016 Ossabaw Island for 1845 Walden Pond, both places convey a common aesthetic of wildness. North End has the largest congregation of buildings and human inhabitants, yet it still presents a wild side. Crumbling buildings and overgrown landscape architecture indicate that nature is hard at work reclaiming the landscape. Such a process takes place slowly, leaving the built environment with an abandoned feeling.

For those who remember the island when it was more heavily inhabited, the sensory experience of returning evokes strong memories. Torrey Kingry, a great-niece of island matriarch Sandy West, first visited in the 1960s. When she has returned to the island over the years, the distinct smell of the marsh reminds her of the place. According to Torrey, the smell is so identifiable that a blind person would have no trouble knowing they had arrived at the landing. Although the nose quickly becomes desensitized to the smell, pluff mud along the inlets and tidal creeks brings the smell of the marsh deep within the island. When returning to the island, it is a potent and early sensation that carries with it the memories of the place.

Recurring sounds, or "keynotes," also leave distinct memories of the place. Except when interrupted by a sudden noise, birds and a breeze are the background notes of the island. Changes to this soundscape made for memories. Carol Burdick, codirector of the Ossabaw Island Project from 1979–1982, recalled an eerie feeling at night. "The pigs ran around making terrible noises at night," and the seventy or eighty donkeys "were very noisy." Likewise, Torrey participated in the Genesis Project at Middle Place as a college student, and the occasional noises were both startling and isolating. One night early in the project, she listened to a series of terrible screams, like someone being murdered in a nearby tent. Although only four miles away from the Main House, the alien

"Barnacle tree"

sounds made Torrey feel much farther away from the island's normal soundscape. It was not until the next day Torrey learned what had taken place: a minx had caught and eaten one of the chickens. The raw sounds of nature made Torrey homesick. For days she longed for the security and quietude of North End.

If not all the sounds of nature were comforting, not all human noises on Ossabaw were unwelcome. Certain human sounds mingled with the sounds of nature in a harmony as if to say that these two forces were not wholly incompatible. Thoreau had remarked on a similar phenomenon in nineteenth-century New England. For him, the tolling of church bells in nearby towns or the chopping of an axe complemented rather than grated against the sounds of nature. In a similar way on Ossabaw, Torrey recalled that a fence and gate protected the Main House's garden from deer and hogs, and cars made a distinctive clunking sound as they passed over the gate's cattle guard. Just as the smell of the pluff mud signaled the arrival at the island, the sounds of the cattle guard marked the arrival at the Main House. Likewise, the acoustics of the Main House's dining room, chief herdsman Roger Parker's "yip, yip, yip" call to his cattle,

Juvenile yellow-crowned night-heron

and the dinner bell were all keynotes—sounds that located someone in a particular time and place—on the island.

When conservationists and scientists have worried about the individual and cumulate effect of human actions on the environment, the senses have often been used as a way to express big fears. In 1962, biologist Rachel Carson issued a call to action against pesticides and herbicides. While the sensory aesthetic of wildness was not new, it was in peril. Even Carson's book title, *Silent Spring*, warned of the auditory signs of trouble ahead. Carson's introduction, "A Fable for Tomorrow," predicted an acoustic desert in a dystopian future. "There was a strange stillness," she wrote, "The birds, for example—where had they gone?" Carson warned that deathly silence would be the ultimate price of pesticides. "On the mornings that had once throbbed with the dawn chorus of robins," she continued, "catbirds, doves, jays, wrens, and scores of other bird voices there was now no sound; only silence lay over the fields and woods and marsh." Springs as silent as the grave would mark the extinction of bird species as well as humanity's own uncertain future.

If it were expressed as its own fable, Ossabaw might foreshadow a brighter, louder future. It is a testament to nature's endurance that an island that has had so many different layers of human history can still exude wildness itself. On multiple occasions, humans have cleared most of the island's forest for timber, or for land, to force slaves to produce commodities, or for space for cattle to graze. People, including Native Americans, planters, slaves, freedmen, Northern industrialists, ranchers, and members of the Georgia Department of Natural Resources, have invested enormous amounts of labor into shaping the island. Ossabaw exemplifies how natural forces act alongside—sometimes in concert with, and sometimes in opposition to—human ones.

Wood storks in the marsh

Pelicans

Western sandpipers at the marsh

Tri-colored heron

Marsh hen

Juvenile white ibis at Willows Roa

Great horned owl

Wood stork

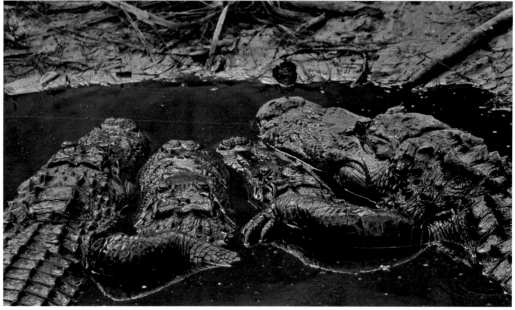

American alligators

Eastern diamondback rattlesnake

Indigo snake

Grasshopper

Butterfly

Deer at High Causeway

Coral bean

Turkey tail mushrooms

Roger Parker on front steps of Main House

3

Changes on the Island
Varieties of Labor

IT WAS 10:30 P.M. WHEN ROGER CAME TO CHECK HIS HOG TRAPS. *He had placed the wooden boxes—approximately five-feet tall, four-feet wide, and seven-feet long—at carefully selected locations. For bait, Roger used a sour-mash mixture created by fermenting a combination of corn and water. The human nose might detect the mixture from twenty yards away. Hogs, however, were known to be able to sense some odors a distance of five miles. Repelling to Roger (at least before distillation), the smell of soured corn was irresistible for hogs.*

Trapped hogs reacted in different ways. Some squealed and growled and pushed against the side of the pen. Others concerned themselves with eating as much sour mash as possible. Roger caught all ages and sizes of hogs. The smaller ones he transferred to pens to raise in captivity. The larger ones might weigh around 150 pounds. Some of these hogs were tenacious descendants of the transatlantic exchange of microbes, animals, and humans that reached Ossabaw by the late sixteenth century. Once introduced by the Spanish, hogs flourished on Ossabaw in cohabitation with or, in other periods, without a resident human population. The Torrey family attempted to eliminate the feral hogs from the island and replace them with a modern domesticated breed in the 1930s, but the genes of Spanish hogs are likely still wandering the island. When Roger and the hog looked eye-to-eye, it was the convergence of paths hundreds of years in the making.

The scene could have happened any night in Roger's five-decade tenure as chief herdsman. Approximately 1,500 feral hogs lived on the island by the early 1970s. A population this size reached a density of six hogs per acre on dry land at high tide. And Roger thought the population might be higher. He certainly never ran out of stock even when, at the heyday of his operation, he trapped seven or eight hundred hogs per year. He was also careful not to overhunt them because doing so would cost him one of his job duties and an additional source of income. After backing his truck up to the trap, Roger herded a trapped hog into a trailer and transported it to a holding pen on North End before transporting it off the island. This live-trap-and-removal program sold hogs to shooting preserves across Georgia and the southeastern states.

Individual nights spent trapping hogs blended together for Roger. It was part of the routine work. He often checked traps multiple times throughout the day and night. The first night check might take place several hours after sundown, around 10:00 or 11:00 P.M. A second check occurred early in the morning, around 4:00 A.M. Resetting the trap doubled his potential gain.

Roger's schedule also speaks to his work rhythm, which set him apart from the more common schedules in post-industrial America. He had a dual sense of time. In the 1970s, he kept meticulous notes about what time he started working, what he accomplished throughout the day, and what time he went home. However, many of his duties went beyond the workday. On the island, clock time mattered less than the daily and weekly rhythms of the island: the ocean tides, the animals, and weather patterns. According to his granddaughter, Amanda, Roger had a sixth sense for knowing when

Wetlands off South End Beach Road

Feral hog

a farm animal was about to go into labor. During these times, Roger checked on the animals at least hourly. He even delivered Mary Helen, one of the island's feral donkeys, who still years later follows Roger around.

Visitors to the island experience at least some of this temporal reorientation. David McCord, a correctional social worker in 1970, witnessed measurable changes in the behavior of at-risk youth he brought to the island. "I began to see people relate to each other as human beings rather than as labels," he wrote. "Ossabaw has that capacity to draw people closer to the real rhythm of life."

When Roger goes to the island he goes to work. He will tell you that only a fraction of the people who like to visit the island could stand the work of the place. His comments point to historical change that he witnessed in his own lifetime. For most of its history, Ossabaw has been a place of hard work, sometimes free and sometimes unfree. Just as the lifecycle of cordgrass has left layers of sediment along the island's marshes, the human management of the island can be conceptualized as a series of successive layers of land and resource use.

THE NATIVE COAST
(4000 BP–1750)

HUMANS HAVE INHABITED THE SOUTHEASTERN ATLANTIC COAST
for more than 10,000 years Before Present (BP), and the oldest permanent settlements on Ossabaw date to about 4,000 years BP. The biodiversity of the marshes
and tidal creeks made Ossabaw an ideal place to fish and gather oysters, shrimp,
crabs, and other shellfish as well as the larger animals also supported by the low-
country. There were also large predators on the island, including red wolves,
black bears, and panthers. As author James Kilgo imagines prehistoric Ossabaw,
"The wet-dog smell of bear mixed with the musk of cat would have charged the
breeze with odor, and the howling of the wolves would have set the air aquiver."
Moreover, the indigenous yaupon holly made the island a place to collect the
ingredients for making a strong emetic tea used in ritual purifications. With a
few exceptions—a drop in sea levels 2,800 to 2,600 years BP forced inhabitants
to rely on other sources of food on land—plant and animal resources abounded.
Reliable sources of coastal food, supplemented in later centuries by the development of agriculture, led to complex social stratification and economic networks
that stretched far beyond the Atlantic coast.

When the Spanish arrived along the southeastern coast of North America
in the sixteenth century, the region was already in flux. Gaule Indians inhabited
pockets of the present-day Georgia coast south of Ossabaw. The island itself,
along with large stretches of land, had been abandoned by the sixteenth century
as a result of failures in agriculture. Large predators, except alligators, were gone
by the time Europeans arrived. In the larger region, waves of European influx
precipitated even greater demographic changes. Epidemics, which often followed
trade routes, decimated the Native American population even before the physical arrival of Europeans. French and Spanish efforts to Christianize the Indians

Drive up to Club House

eroded social order, and the English mercantile system wiped out nearly all those remaining. By about 1700, the Muskogeans, or Creeks, had established a presence on Ossabaw, and they retained nominal hunting and fishing rights for decades. In the place of a permanent human population, feral hogs began taking over the island.

THE PLANTATION ENVIRONMENT
(1750–1861)

A NEW LAYER OF LAND USE TOOK SHAPE IN THE SECOND HALF of the eighteenth century. The human presence on the island increased again with the rise of slavery in the colony and, later, the state. While Georgia's Trustees originally banned slavery in the 1730s, they lifted the ban in 1750. The natural bounty that attracted Native Americans to live on the island brought profit-minded planters to produce commodities including timber, indigo, rice, and cotton. John Morel of Savannah, together with his father-in-law, purchased Ossabaw at auction in 1760 and began commodifying the island's resources. In 1770, he advertised in the *Georgia Gazette* that any quantity, shape, and size of live oak and cedar timber could be purchased from his land on Ossabaw. One ship, named the *Bewlie*, was built at the Beaulieu shipyard near Savannah; another, the *Elizabeth*, was built on Ossabaw itself from the island's timber stores.

The idea of permanently residing within a sea island environment did not appeal to many plantation owners by the nineteenth century. White physicians thought decomposing plant and animal matter produced *miasmas* (an unpleasant smell) and *malaria* (literally meaning "bad air"), which caused disease. The presence of malaria near swamps and newly cleared lowlands, which, in retrospect, can be understood as coming not from the smell of swamps but from the bite of

mosquitoes, meant that those with the ability to do so avoided low-country wet-lands and marshes.

For more than 100 years, enslaved people made up the vast majority of humans on Ossabaw. From the planter's perspective, this was a logical solution to the environmental problem. Whites also justified enslavement through the senses. Stereotypes that buttressed slavery often called on the senses as evidence of white superiority and black inferiority. Whites generally assumed blacks had thicker skin and a duller sense of touch than themselves, which justified hard manual labor and corporal punishment by the lash. Physicians believed that "hands," as planters and overseers called enslaved people, were less susceptible than whites to those diseases endemic to foul-smelling, low-country environ-ments. When enslaved people put up resistance by regularly breaking tools to slow down work, it reinforced the planter's belief in their innate clumsiness. To curb the cost of replacing tools, planters ordered overseers to keep track of tools and hold regular inspections, the volumes of which are preserved for at least one Ossabaw plantation. In this way, slaveholders justified and naturalized slavery, at least in part, through the senses.

Planters sent large populations of enslaved laborers under the discipline of white overseers to tend to crops that grew well in the fertile low-country. In 1800, Chatham County, which included Ossabaw Island and Savannah, had a population of 3,673 whites, 9,049 enslaved blacks, and 224 free blacks. Seventy percent of the people living in Chatham County, and nearly everyone living on Ossabaw, were enslaved. In the 1850s, there were about 225 enslaved people living on the four plantations on Ossabaw Island.

George Kollock exemplified the absentee style of management utilized by most planters on Ossabaw. A lawyer turned plantation owner, Kollock pur-chased 800 acres on Ossabaw Island in 1848. He lived hundreds of miles away in the upstate, near Clarkesville, Georgia. Although he made trips to Savannah

Southern live oak near Middle Place

Club House

and the island to appraise the values of cotton and corn, he left day-to-day plantation management to white overseers whom he gave authority to enforce strict discipline. On the mainland in 1840 and 1841, Kollock directed white overseers that slaves should not "receive more than ten lashes unless I am present." In 1842, Kollock increased that number to twenty lashes. Overseers on Ossabaw likely had similar authority. One enslaved man on Ossabaw named Lee missed four days of work in 1849 after a severe beating by overseer J. W. Gillam. Kollock expected every "hand" to be in the field at sunrise unless the overseer judged that the man or woman had an adequate excuse for absence. Yet Kollock worried about the rigors of the island on his own health. On a visit in May 1852, he thought himself prudent for waiting until after dinner to inspect the fields. It was too much of a risk to expose his delicate, white skin to the harsh rays of the sun in a disease-prone environment.

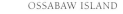

The Ossabaw experience was also divided by taste. In the eighteenth and nineteenth centuries, elites in Europe and the Americas argued that animals fed, humans ate, and only the refined had a true sense of taste. As with the sense of touch, whites argued that black people had a duller sense of taste. This belief was self-serving as it justified providing only the most basic rations to enslaved people. Kollock, for example, directed that slaves bring provisions, probably coarse cornmeal, and cooking pots into the field and allowed them two hours in the summer and one hour in the winter to cook their own rations. Enslaved people probably supplemented their rations with vegetables from small gardens as well as oysters, fish, raccoons, and hogs from the island. White planters such as Kollock, who had more self-described refined tastes, experienced the island in a different way. When his imported food stores ran low in May 1852, Kollock directed his wife to send him wheat bread and butter. He also sent for wine glasses because "eggs do not eat so well out of tumblers as they do out of wine glasses."

The plantation system established a new political, social, and economic framework on Ossabaw and brought severe ecological changes to the island's landscape. Enslaved people dug ditches and drained ponds for rice cultivation. Large sections of the island's forests were cut away for cotton fields. In 1850, one of George Kollock's slaves spent ninety-four days cutting cordgrass in Ossabaw's marshes. Others transported large amounts of mud from the marshes to fertilize the cotton fields. Under the orders of Kollock and other planters, much of the island was clear-cut, with the exception of some of the old-growth live oaks, to make room for commercial crops, food crops for the enslaved population, and grazing land for livestock.

THE LIMITS OF RECONSTRUCTION
(1861–1900)

EARLY IN THE CIVIL WAR, WHITE LANDOWNERS ABANDONED Ossabaw Island. The collapse of the plantation economy between 1861 and 1865 led to a new historical layer on Ossabaw. The period after emancipation was marked by dreams of small independent farms, dashed first by political and later by natural forces. Special Orders No. 15, issued by Union general William T. Sherman in January 1865, enabled the army to redistribute land along the Atlantic coast from Charleston, South Carolina, to the St. John's River in Florida. Tunis G. Campbell, an agent of the federal government's Bureau of Refugees, Freedmen, and Abandoned Lands—known as the "Freedmen's Bureau"—oversaw five Sea Islands. He was charged with the responsibility of helping former slaves establish a local government. By August 1865, sixteen African American families held promissory titles to a total of 345 acres of land on the former plantations on Ossabaw's North End, Middle Place, and South End.

Tabby-walled slave quarters

Interior of slave quarters

After this initial redistribution, President Andrew Johnson began the undoing of black land ownership on Ossabaw by pardoning former Confederates and limiting the powers of the Freedmen's Bureau. By 1867, former slaveholders had regained formal possession of all their land on Ossabaw Island. The situation on Ossabaw was tense, with people's livelihoods at stake. In January 1867 the *General Shepley*, a steamer docked at Ossabaw to receive cotton, went up in flames. Newspapers in Savannah attributed it to African Americans on Ossabaw who feared there was a conspiracy to kidnap and remove them to a different country, such as Cuba or Brazil, where slavery was still legal. Similar things had happened before. Black families with the means to do so left the island in search of property on the mainland. Unlike Sapelo and St. Simons islands, where former enslaved people were able to buy land, those who stayed on Ossabaw did so as sharecroppers.

Nature provided the final undoing. The African Americans who stayed on Ossabaw owned no land, but they lived there as a small community for the

Detail, tabby wall

next three decades. Residents named their Baptist church "Hinder Me Not," in reference to a verse in the biblical book Genesis. The name exemplified the feelings of those who survived slavery and the feelings of betrayal by the government policies during Reconstruction. The Zion Baptist Association admitted the Hinder Me Not Church in 1874, and at its peak, the church had a membership of sixty-eight worshipers. Although membership numbers had been dropping already in the 1890s, a series of hurricanes in 1896 and 1898 pushed remaining families to the mainland. The strongest of these storms made landfall south of Ossabaw on Cumberland Island on October 2, 1898, causing severe damage all along the Georgia coast. As of spring 2016, it was the last major hurricane to hit the Georgia coastline.

The storms finished what the collapse of plantation agriculture and rise in sharecropping had started. The Hinder Me Not Church and community left Ossabaw for the mainland, where its descendants still attend Sweetfield of Eden

Baptist Church and First Beulah Baptist Church near Savannah.
In 1900, only six people, four white and two black, lived on
Ossabaw.

WILDERNESS AND HUNTING LODGES
(1900–1924)

AS PLANTATION AGRICULTURE COLLAPSED during the
American Civil War and the island's human population declined
over the rest of the century, nature began covering up some evidence of human alterations. It was not that people no longer used
the land, but they used it in a different way. Gone were fields,
perhaps hundreds of acres, of cleared agricultural land. In their
place were reemerging forests—good places for the descendants
of Spanish hogs to root for sustenance. By the 1920s, an esti-
mated 5,000 deer, 2,000 wild cattle, and 10,000 boars lived on the
island.

Subdivided in the nineteenth century, the island's ownership was still fragmented by the early twentieth century. Henry
Davis Weed, a merchant from Savannah and the son of the
president of the Savannah Bank and Trust Company, began the
reconsolidation process. The reason for doing so was probably
financial and personal. Weed purchased three-fourths of the island
in 1906. Ten years later, in March 1916, he purchased the fourth
portion, and, six days later, resold the island as a single unit. Yet
Weed also loved hunting, and he sold the island to a group of
businessmen who shared this desire to use the entire island as a

Tower House at Middle Place

hunting retreat. The owners hired a superintendent to take care of the island and a pack of hunting dogs. Parts of the island were rented to small farmers, but the population on the island remained low during this period. In 1920, only twenty-three people in five households lived on the island.

FROM HUNTING RETREAT
TO NATURE PRESERVE
(1924–1978)

FOR THE FIRST GENERATION OF THE TORREY FAMILY'S OWNERSHIP, the land-use strategy reflected that of the hunters. When Dr. Henry Norton Torrey (1880–1945) purchased the entire island in 1924, it came near the end of an era when Northern industrialists bought up Southern Sea Islands. The Torreys had previously owned a mansion, "Greenwich," on the Wilmington River near Savannah that burned in 1923. When the Torreys purchased Ossabaw, they continued to live in Detroit, Michigan, for most of the year but retreated to the island between January and May.

For many decades, the Torrey family utilized the island's resources for both leisure and profit. Mounds of sawdust at Middle Place, South End, and elsewhere indicate a continuing presence of the timber industry through the early '60s. As the island passed from one generation to another, assumptions about the value of the island's natural resources changed as well. Sandy Torrey West inherited half of the island in 1959 and her late brother's children the other half. This new generation of the Torrey family grew up visiting the island in the winters and recognized the greater ecological value of the island rather than emphasizing only its economic value. Major changes followed. The family eventually put a stop to logging and turned away mineral-extracting companies. A cattle and pig ranching operation would be the only source of income from the land. Although the island had never regained the population density it had during its plantation era, the Torreys restricted where people could live to two locations on the island: North End and Middle Place.

Sandy led by example. In 1961, she and her husband, Clifford, took additional steps in conserving the island. They conceptualized and funded the Ossabaw Island Project, which encouraged the use of the island for interdisciplinary collaboration, research, and exploration. There was an element of experimentation and radicalism about it. According to Al Bradford, one of the codirectors of the Ossabaw Island Project, Sandy's projects were analogous to her viewpoint about the relationship between people, animals, and nature. Sandy loves Ossabaw, Bradford argues, because "animals can be themselves there. They can be wild animals there instead of being penned up and being in a zoo or being on a farm." From this perspective, the purpose of the Ossabaw Island Project was to let humans learn to be themselves.

While many guests came to the island to research and work on creative projects, Ossabaw never stopped being a place of labor. The artists and writers who used the island for inspiration relied on the island's eighteen-person workforce, white and black, to make the projects possible. Those who ran the projects were not always sensitive to the class and racial lines that divided the visiting artists from the workers. Carol Burdick, codirector of the Ossabaw Project, recalled "the island people who were responsible for running the island, for running the boats, for [cutting] the wood, for doing the housework were a new breed for me to meet also." All the food was prepared by the island's cooks. Describing the white and black cooks, Burdick continued, "Queen[ie] or Mable or Agnes would ring the big bell, and if you weren't there in five or ten minutes of the bell, you might find your grits were passed along the table.... And they were good breakfasts!" Participants went off to work on their own projects and returned around noon to pick up a lunch. A dinner bell rang again at 6:30 P.M. to bring the participants back to the Main House, followed by coffee in the living room "so that the women could get the dishes done and get home to their own families." The creative breakthroughs visitors achieved were only possible because the island remained a place of labor for most people.

The most radical change to take place on the island concerned ownership. For 200 years, Ossabaw had been private property and subject to the whims of its owners. In 1963, the island was appraised by the state at between $1,000,000 and $1,250,000. In 1965, the Torrey family received an offer of $1,000,000 from a private investor and $1,500,000 from a conservation group, but at the time they were not ready to sell to anyone. By the end of the decade, though, the Torrey family faced a financial dilemma and a difficult decision. In 1969, Chatham County reappraised the island for tax purposes at $2,659,150. As a result, annual property taxes on the island rose from $5,000 to $48,000. The family appealed the appraisal, and the ensuing arbitration lowered the annual taxes in 1971 to $28,740. While Sandy came from a very wealthy family, she had very little income. Unable to hold onto the island forever, she sought to sell the island to someone who would keep it wild in perpetuity. When the island passed from private ownership to public ownership in 1978, the subject of chapter 5, it entered a new era in its history.

Tower House at Middle Place

OSSABAW ISLAND
· ·
94

One of Roger's fences at slave quarters

Overseer's house at Middle Place

Portrait of Sandy as a young girl with her mother and brother, ca. 1920

Main Road

Foggy morning on North End

4

Working Ossabaw

FOR ROGER'S SON, GRAYLING, AND GRANDDAUGHTER, AMANDA, *Ossabaw evokes a range of emotions. When Roger moved into one of the old tabby slave quarters in 1970, Grayling began calling the island home at the age of twelve. Grayling thinks of the island in nearly a mystical sense. He frequently discusses the island as a unified whole with a will and the power to act. Growing up, the island provided turkeys, deer, hogs, shrimp, and fish. Supplementing the island's bounty with a large vegetable garden, Grayling remembers eating very few items from a grocery store. They needed flour, sugar, coffee, and rice, but the island provided everything else. Living on Ossabaw was as close as one could get to subsistence agriculture in the 1970s.*

While Grayling moved to Ossabaw as an adolescent, Amanda's personal connection to the island began even earlier in life. For this reason, she recalls taking the island's uniqueness for granted as a child. Some of her earliest memories come from the island, and it is difficult to disentangle one early memory from another out there. She stayed on the island entire summers and spent most of her weekends there as well. Unlike those who visit the island, she has no clear "first" memory of the place. The island simply has always been a strong part of her life.

Shark sculpture in front of Main House

Living on the island shaped Amanda's and Grayling's early views of the rest of the world. As a child, Amanda assumed that most people visited islands, rode horses, and helped their grandfathers check hog traps at night. She assumed that all televisions cut out at about 3:00 P.M., the time when her grandfather happened to check the generator each afternoon. The sight of a skinned animal or the smell of sour cornmeal in a hog trap were normal parts of everyday life. Relationships to the island became more complicated when Amanda began going to school. During the school year, Amanda caught the bus at the marina, just as Grayling had done for years, and in both instances it led to the expected teasing from classmates. During inclement weather in the 1970s, classmates took bets on whether Grayling would show up at the marina—a bet Grayling took a small cut from when he invariably showed up. The friends Amanda made were those whose parents were willing to let them ride several miles by boat to spend weekends on a farm. In short, there were social costs, and it took the passage of time to appreciate some of the unique qualities of the island. Living on an island had benefits, but it also resulted in some feelings of isolation and being "different."

Everyone in the family worked; no one had a free ride. Roger's wife, Sarah, worked for Sandy in the Main House and later piloted boats back and forth from the mainland. Grayling frequently helped his father with various tasks on the farm. Killing deer, trapping hogs, mending fences, and working with cattle were part of the rhythm of daily life. Amanda grew up in eager anticipation of the day when she could help her grandfather. Her first job was porting the luggage of visitors on their way to the Main House. When Amanda was twelve, Roger increased her responsibilities by allowing her to drive his yellow Datsun truck on the island. One of her favorite tasks, though, was helping Roger clean hogs. The work was not always easy, but working with her grandfather made for rich memories.

The family witnessed big changes on the island. When Roger started working there in 1951, there was no reason to think it would ever be anything other than a farm. When Amanda has returned to the island, one noticeable change is the quietude on the

North End. An underwater power line has replaced the diesel generators that provided electricity for the island until the 1990s. Before this change, generators could be heard over much of the north end of the island. In Roger's home video collection, a whirring sound dominates as a background noise on certain parts of North End.

Other changes, such as differing opinions about the Department of Natural Resources' management policies, are less pleasant. Watching Roger's last cattle leave the island in 1990 signified the end of an era. Since that time, the island's horses, turkeys, and peacocks have died off, and the feral donkey population, which the Department of Natural Resources sterilized, will soon follow. Maintenance of the roads and bridges is also a major concern. They were carefully maintained during Roger's tenure. While Roger seems to be immune to this sort of sentimentality, watching the effects of nature on Roger's roads and fences is more troubling for Grayling and Amanda. And, finally, the island represents a longstanding relationship between a wealthy landowner and labor that has not always been pleasant. Verbal agreements indicated that Roger would receive a pension for his sixty years of work, but that never materialized when Sandy ran into financial problems. When Roger's formal career on the island ended, it divided feelings about the relationship to the island.

TODAY, THE WORD "COWBOY" CONJURES UP IMAGES of a man on horseback in a Western setting. Is the nickname "Saltwater Cowboy," then, a stretch? Not really. Roger's work and nickname have deep roots along the southeastern coast. By the mid-eighteenth century, large numbers of feral cattle grazed the open spaces of Georgia. Carolina "black cattle" wandered into Georgia from large herds north of the Savannah River, where by 1700 more than half of the male

Bay window, Main House

slaves in the colony were listed as "cattle hunters," or cowboys. Spanish cattle moved north from parts of Florida. On the mainland along rivers, in marshes, and on coastal islands, cattle found sufficient forage to increase quickly in population. There were cowboys along the southeastern coast 150 years before the "Old West."

When Roger imagined the future as a child, he probably foresaw a life working with his hands. Raised in a ranching family near Richmond Hill, Georgia, he grew up performing hard work on a regular basis with his father, Arthur, born in the preceding century and a farmer himself since finishing primary school. In 1940, when Roger was 4 years old, Arthur headed a family of eight, worked fifty-two weeks a year, and reported $1,000 in income, the equivalent in 2016 dollars of about $17,000. Roger did not graduate from high school. During his high school years, he found basketball and farm work more appealing. It was a challenging but rewarding life on the intersection of nature and civilization.

Although Roger first spent the night on the island in 1951, he began working there on a regular basis in 1953 at age 18. Working on the island was something of a family tradition. Two of Roger's uncles, Eugene and Arthur Graves, were island managers before Roger took over. Roger's brother, Stanfield, served as a mechanic on vehicles and boats. He had aunts who worked in the Main House. Roger's family members were part of a network of men and women, white and black, who worked the island, including James Brownlee, Queenie Mae Williams, Richard Boaen, Cyrus "Jimbo" Martin, Agnes Graves Moody, and Liz Graves. Some years Roger stayed on the island more than others, and when he got married in early 1964, he divided his time between the island and the mainland because his son, Grayling, needed to be closer to school. During the early years on the island, Roger lived upstairs with his aunt and uncle at the Boarding House.

Roger Parker, 2016

On April Fool's Day 1970, Roger moved into one of the old tabby slave quarters with his wife and son. He spent ten hours that first day working on the tabby tenant house that became his family's home for years to come. The building's previous tenants, also workers on the island, had been rough on the place. The floorboards were damaged, and with great difficulty Roger removed the smell of pet hamsters from the house. Roger spent months making the tabby house comfortable, but his job did not leave much time for settling into the new place. On the second day, he helped raise a recently sunken barge. On the third day, he helped get a truck out of a ditch, picked up a group of college students at the southernmost landing, worked on his house, and filled a fuel tank.

Farm equipment and vehicles on the island required constant maintenance. An old Ford tractor gave Roger considerable trouble. For the first two weeks after moving to the island, Roger spent more time fixing the tractor than driving it. Roger let nothing go to waste, but it was clear to him that the tractor had to go. After struggling with it for a year, he bought a new one, which he has kept in working order now for more than forty years. Vehicles were another consistent trouble. In May 1970, Roger got a flat tire on a Chevy pickup truck shortly after 8 A.M. Then, as if on cue, the spare tire became flat too. Roger carefully drove the limping truck to the shop, where he spent the rest of the morning working on it. Late that fall, the truck broke down miles from home near South End Beach. "We could not get it to start," Roger wrote, "so we stayed there until someone came to look for us." Luckily, within two hours, several of the other workers did come looking for them. Trucks also became mired in the mud on a regular basis, sometimes multiple times on the same day.

Dirt roads require a great deal of maintenance. The biggest threat to dirt roads is water. In tidally influenced areas, an abnormally high tide washes out a road with ease. In such areas, the force of water is nearly irresistible, and keeping roads serviceable requires constant effort. In other areas, care must be taken to

Roger and Sandy

Generator buildings; facing page, Main House courtyard

minimize and delay the effect of rainwater. A slight curvature to a road and a drainage ditch softens the effects of a hard rain. Lacking gravel, broken oyster shells, left over from Native American shell middens, offered a valuable substitute. Before island ownership transferred to the state, truckloads of these shells were collected to cover the roads.

Roger's cattle-herding and pig-trapping took up even more of his time. When cattle roamed the island freely, Roger had to patrol the edges of the high ground to make sure no animals became bogged down in the marshes. Although initially free range, by the 1970s Roger had to maintain a series of fences around the island, especially at Buckhead, Middle Place, and North End. After the state of Georgia purchased the island in 1978, the Department of Natural Resources began pushing for the ultimate removal of cattle from the island. Roger removed the last cattle from Ossabaw in 1990.

From 1970 until 1982, Roger worked not only with the animals but also with the visiting scholars in the Ossabaw Island Project and the students in the Genesis Project. This was not always easy. Cultural difference cut both directions.

Hallway to courtyard, Main House

Carol Burdick, codirector of the Ossabaw Island Project, described how she had to change her approach in working with "island people." She learned, for example, "You don't just go and say, 'Roger, I need this.' You say, 'Hiya, Roger. How are you today? What do you think of the weather today? Well, I was wondering if you'd have any time to….'" And Roger was not the only worker on the island Carol sometimes struggled to relate to. Queenie Mae Williams, who worked on the island for decades, knew that Carol went by her initials, C. B., but Queenie referred to her as FBI—a subtle joke that hinted at the underlying tension.

Although most of the time Roger was working—and working hard—on Ossabaw, there were regular celebrations as well. Carol described these events, like the rest of the island, as "wild." In the late '70s and early '80s, there were barbeques at Roger and Sarah's house on North End every six weeks or so. Friends of Roger and Sarah who did occasional road, farm, mechanical, or boat work for the island would come over from the mainland. "The numbers would swell," Carol recalled, "and you'd find yourself in the middle of a real Southern

Sunroom, Main House

barbeque." The fare usually consisted of barbeque pork and venison, and par-tygoers turned the backs of trucks into bars. "There would be dogs yapping for bones at the edge of the spotlit yard…. The music would be loud, the moon would be shining, and everybody loved it."

Roger no longer formally works for Sandy West, but he still goes to Ossabaw to volunteer. Driving that same tractor he purchased in 1970 to pull a log splitter, Roger cuts firewood and fat lighter (highly flammable resin-filled wood from pine trees) for the Main House and for his own use in the small ranch-style house nearby. He argues that he can still do everything he used to do, even if it takes more time now and requires a little help from his closest friends, Everette and Shawn Boaen, Trey Coursey, and Allen Usher. Roger's old friends have regularly accompanied him to exchange six or seven hours of work a day for the opportunity to visit such a unique place. The time between stretches of hard work on Ossabaw is worth the toil. The opportunities for fishing are remind-ers of Ossabaw's past and present natural bounty. Walks down the old roads are reminders of the place's deep human and natural history.

Dining room, Main House

Kitchen, Main House

Kitchen, Main House

Great room, Main House

Great room, Main House

Great room, Main House

"Blue Room," Main House

"Magic Room," Main House

Richard's room, Main House

Bathroom, Main House

Sandy's horse, "Poco"

Foggy morning on the marsh

Front yard at Main House

5

Preserving Wildness

GRAYLING CAME OF AGE ON OSSABAW ISLAND during the last eight years Sandy West owned the island, when there were still eighteen paid employees living there. Ossabaw was a working island. He remembers the Ossabaw Island Project and the Genesis Project, which brought scholars and free spirits to rural Georgia, as well as the changes that came with the transition from private to public ownership. When he looks at the tabby slave quarters today, he recalls how different they looked in the 1970s. The tabby walls were the core of a much larger building with a kitchen and a master bedroom. By highlighting one layer of the building's history—the antebellum architecture—the building today shows no indication it was lived in until only a few decades ago. Preservation requires choices that can obscure as well as reveal different layers of the past.

In a similar way, Grayling has mixed feelings about the re-wilding of the island's modern management. Although protected from private development, the establishment of Ossabaw as a state heritage preserve means that it is no longer a working island. He remembers a freshly painted Main House with a well-manicured lawn. Grayling refers to this type of maintenance as "keeping her face clean," by which he means the face of Ossabaw. Today the roads are in bad need of repair. Changing currents, rising sea levels, and higher than normal tides have washed out parts of many of the roads. For Grayling, it is a reminder that Ossabaw has passed into a new layer of history.

THIS CONCLUDING CHAPTER TRACES THE RECENT HISTORY of the island within the context of environmental and historic preservation movements of the last fifty years. Between 1978 and 2012, the Georgia Department of Natural Resources came to manage 429,000 acres of land. While Georgia has fewer acres of public land than other Southern states, Ossabaw Island represents an important success story about public-private partnerships. Questions about the management and future of the island remain. Although related, the priorities of environmental and historic preservation sometimes conflict. Could protecting one resource come at the expense of the other?

From a longer view, the protection of Ossabaw Island represents the coming of age of two interrelated movements: one to preserve nature and another to manage cultural resources. Both movements required action by individuals, nonprofits, and all levels of government. At the same time Sandy West and the Torrey family began reconsidering how to utilize Ossabaw Island, major national changes were taking place in the valuation of environmental and cultural resources. The impulse for the protection of nature and culture were similar: in an age of rapid growth, the bulldozer came to symbolize both the promise and the threat of progress. In Georgia, odor was also a symbol. To some, pulp and paper mills smelled like jobs and economic vitality. To others, the same

Crab traps and cars at the Island dump

rotten-egg smell symbolized the loss of artesian wells and other forms of environmental degradation. One thing was certain: economic development had the potential to lead to the loss of important natural habitats as well as historic architecture and archaeological sites. In response to the bulldozer revolution after World War II, a counter-revolution emerged emphasizing natural stewardship and historic preservation.

Response came from both the bottom up and the top down. At the national level, the National Historic Preservation Act of 1966 and the National Environmental Protection Act of 1969 marked positive steps toward ensuring that possible adverse effects of federally funded or licensed projects would be considered. In the 1970s, Georgia passed two important bills affecting natural resources. The Coastal Marshlands Protection Act, passed in 1970 and amended in 1992, applies to 700,000 acres of estuarine areas and is designed to prevent undertakings from altering the natural flow of water, increasing erosion, or causing adverse effects on marine life. Any projects that have the potential to cause adverse effects on these areas require a permit from the Coastal Marshlands Protection Committee. A second influential Georgia law, the Shore Protection Act of 1979, set out to regulate activities and construction projects that could disturb sand dunes and beaches.

Bookended by these two state laws, the 1970s witnessed strong leadership in environmental protection. In his inaugural address as governor of Georgia, Jimmy Carter followed his pronouncement "that the time for racial discrimination is over" with an additional challenge. "Georgia is a state of great natural beauty and promise," he said, "but the quality of our natural surroundings

"Automotive Graveyard"

is threatened because of avarice, selfishness, procrastination and neglect." While Carter agreed that change and development benefited the state, he warned, "Our challenge is to ensure that such activities avoid destruction and dereliction of our environment." As governor, Carter spent much time protecting natural resources through state acquisition and boldly vetoed a proposal to build the Sprewell Bluff Dam along the Flint River. Governor Carter gained national attention for his environmental achievements for these efforts.

As president, Jimmy Carter continued to promote sound environmental policies. Having learned the value of bold executive action as governor, Carter protected sensitive ecosystems such as wetlands and deserts from the Oval Office. He began farsighted planning for alternative and renewable energy sources, created the Department of Energy, and started the Environmental Protection Agency's "Superfund" program to clean up areas polluted by toxic waste. Lastly, the Alaska Lands Act, passed in December 1980, vastly expanded the total area of national parks and wilderness lands.

Working into the final days of his term in office, President Carter set an example of natural resource stewardship that encouraged others to act within their power to protect the environment, including Sandy West and the Torrey family. While state and federal lawmakers organized a legal system to curb adverse effects of projects on cultural and natural resources, local governments, nonprofit organizations, and individual citizens began their own efforts to protect urban and rural landscapes. On Ossabaw, this began with a changing educational mission. While the Ossabaw Island Project focused on opening an inspiring place to established artists and intellectuals, the Genesis Project (1970–1982) used the outdoor setting as a classroom for youths undertaking independent projects. There were earlier precursors to this type of outdoor learning experience. In 1969, a group of twenty-five male and female students from Shorter College spent eight days on the island, ending their trip with a dinner at the Main

Roger with his uncle's truck

Sandy's mother's Packard

House and a lecture given by nationally known ecologist Eugene Odum. Genesis immersed students in nature. Participants paid tuition of $10 a week and lived on the island for about three months the first year and two months in following years. Students built their own shelters, raised their own food, and assisted Roger Parker and other island staff in maintaining machinery, roads, boats, and fences. "When you come to Ossabaw Island," one former participant observed, "you have the opportunity for silence." In such stillness lay the opportunity for both personal growth and awareness about land ethics, conservation, and preservation.

After the original Ossabaw Island and Genesis projects ended in the 1980s, other research and educational programs continued into the 1990s and 2000s. The Professional Research Program (which ended in the 1990s) and the Public Use and Education Program have hosted scholars in many fields, including anthropology, archaeology, biology, climatology, veterinary medicine, and wildlife management. The cumulative scope of decades of projects was huge. Nearly 900 scholars from a wide array of disciplines participated in the Ossabaw Island Project alone. And it exemplified a strand of radical thinking not usually associated with a Southern state.

The Torrey family's decision to sell Ossabaw Island to the state of Georgia had the longest lasting effect on the future of the island. The sale was never inevitable. The Fish and Wildlife Service indicated the US government's interest in establishing a wildlife refuge on the island in 1964, but the Torrey family lost interest when they deemed the price too low. As time went on, however, the price of keeping the island in private hands became too great. In December 1972, Governor Carter, Georgia Department of Natural Resources Commissioner Joe Tanner, and a few other officials visited Ossabaw. Carter recalls, "Joe [Tanner] and I looked over the island at her [Sandy West's] request.... We saw what a precious possession she owned and how beneficial it would be to future generations if it

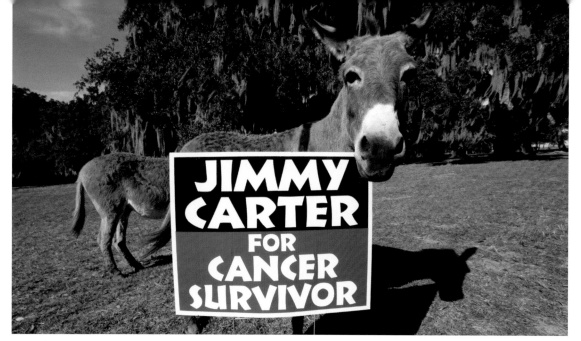

Sandy's donkeys

was protected and not turned over to someone who could buy it at the court-house steps." Although the island produced limited revenue, the value of Sea Islands began to increase rapidly as developers began building large-scale resorts along the Eastern coast. From Carter's perspective, Sandy had only two choices. "One was to sell it to the state and see it preserved not only during her lifetime but in perpetuity," he remembers. Her second option was to sell it to the highest bidder. In a thank-you letter to Sandy, Carter reminder her, "We have a common purpose in ensuring a proper future of the island." Along with this letter he attached a plan outlining an agreement to conserve the island by making it public land. The choice between stewardship and self-interest harkened back to Carter's inaugural address.

Although it took six years to implement the plan from their initial meeting, Sandy chose to put the future of the island ahead of her own finances. In 1978, President Jimmy Carter and former Georgia DNR commissioner Joe Tanner mediated negotiations between Sandy West, the rest of the Torrey family, and the state legislature. The family agreed to sell the island at a negotiated price of $8,000,000, a sum fifty times more than the family paid for it in 1924 but only half its estimated value at the time. Even this sale might have faltered had it not been for a challenge grant made by philanthropist Robert W. Woodruff amounting to half of the sale price. It was a deal of incredible foresight by the Torrey family and the state.

In 1978, Ossabaw Island became the state's first heritage preserve. The Georgia Heritage Trust Act of 1975, passed during Jimmy Carter's term as governor, created the heritage trust program to "preserve important and endangered elements of Georgia's heritage." One month after the island changed hands, Governor George Busbee issued the executive order stating that the island could "only be used for natural, scientific, and cultural study, research and education, and environmentally sound preservation, conservation, and management of the Island's ecosystem." To preserve the island's remoteness, the executive order forbids the construction of a bridge or a paved or lighted landing strip. Changes to the island require action by the Board of Natural Resources, the State Properties Committee, the state governor, or the legislature, and the process must involve public input. The agreement between the Torrey family and the state also set aside a life estate, which included the Main House and 24 acres on the North End, which Sandy West continues to exercise into 2016 at the age of 103.

Although owned and managed by the state of Georgia, the Ossabaw Island Foundation handles educational activities and public access. Established in 1994, the Ossabaw Island Foundation is a 501(c)3 nonprofit organization that operates through an ongoing use agreement with the state. The organization's mission mirrors the executive order establishing Ossabaw as a heritage preserve, maximizing the use of Ossabaw Island's resources for education and research while preserving those same resources from adverse effects.

Since the public-private partnership was established, the Ossabaw Island Foundation has taken the lead in educational programing as well as the preservation on the North End of the island. The organization raised the funds to repair the roof on the Main House and pioneered efforts to research and tell the social history of the island, recovering the voices of enslaved people on the island as well as the workers, both white and black, who lived on the island in the twentieth century. After the row of three tabby slave quarters was identified as a major preservation issue in the 1990s, the organization led the effort to preserve and interpret them. In 2013, Joseph McGill, a reenactor and preservationist with the National Trust for Historic Preservation, spent the night in one of the tabbies as part of his highly publicized Slave Dwelling Project. The organization's preservation, education, and outreach programs promise to bring together cultural resource management and historic site interpretation of the remote island in a comprehensive way.

While the preservation of the standing historic resources on North End has been made a priority, the success of long-term preservation of Middle Place is less assured. With the exception of one tabby building and the ruins of others, extant buildings are not formally considered to be contributing historic resources. This sentiment may change as the buildings become eligible for the National Register of Historic Places when the Genesis Project turns 50 years old in 2020.

Lingering environmental and historic preservation questions surround the Ossabaw Island pigs. On one hand, the Georgia Department of Natural Resources rightfully considers them invasive and destructive to plant and animal life. Hogs tear up the landscape and, as true omnivores, consume nearly everything in their path. They will eat amphibians and reptiles, including endangered sea turtle eggs on the beaches. Although a menace to sensitive resources, the hog population is also a valuable cultural resource, representing hundreds of years of entangled human and natural history as well as a story of adaptation and survival

Sandy's donkeys

Front yard under fog; facing page, artist's studio near Main House

to environmental pressure. Ecologists have noted that Ossabaw hogs acquired the ability to drink water with high salinity and developed a form of noninsulin-dependent diabetes that allows them to survive in a less-than-ideal habitat. Moreover, like the yaupon holly centuries ago, Ossabaw hogs have become an important symbol of the island's taste today. There is a high demand for Ossabaw pigs by chefs and restaurateurs for their denser meat and more flavorsome taste. Roger Parker speculates that the hogs' free-range diet in such an environment makes for a better taste.

A second concluding question about the future of Ossabaw relates back to the five senses. Preservationists usually deal in buildings, in historic fabric, and in a "sense of place," which in practice means visual similarity. Vision creates an illusion of continuity between past and present, just as Ossabaw's regrowth presents the illusion that the island has had little human history. When all the senses are taken into consideration, the meaning of preservation becomes muddy. As the island has changed, the sensory environments that made the Ossabaw experience

Christmas goose

A resourceful raccoon

unique—whether the brutalities of slavery, the ranching uses in the twentieth century, or the island's slow process of taking back its natural landscape—have changed too. In this view, the sensory experience cannot be contained or preserved except perhaps in an episodic way through writing and photographs. Sandy West moved off the island on May 1, 2016, and into an assisted-living home in Savannah. When she passes away, when the DNR possibly removes the last donkeys and hogs from the island, and when the island reclaims the ruins of buildings not slated for preservation, the island will begin to construct yet another layer of its long history. The current layer will be as irretrievable as the ones that came before it, but one thing is certain. The sensory experiences of Ossabaw will always be what make the island special.

Shrimp boat seen from Sandy's front yard

A Short Bibliographic Essay

ALTHOUGH FORMAL FOOTNOTES AND ENDNOTES HAVE BEEN AVOIDED in the final draft of this text, this book stands on the shoulders of local and regional experts. The first comprehensive history of the island is Linda Orr King's dissertation, "An Eccentric Place of Very High Quality: Ossabaw Island, Georgia as a Context for the Interpretation for Historical, Cultural, and Environmental Change on the Atlantic Coast," (PhD diss., Atlanta: Georgia State University, 2015). One of the most accessible published books on Ossabaw Island is Ann Foskey's *Images of America: Ossabaw Island* (Charleston, SC: Arcadia Publishing, 2001). Jane Fishman's *The Woman Who Saved an Island* (Savannah, GA: Real People Publishing, 2014) is also an important starting point for the story of Eleanor (Sandy) Torrey West, and Burnette Vanstory's *Georgia's Land of the Golden Isles* (Athens: University of Georgia Press, 1956) is a useful but dated introduction to the state's Sea Islands. Of the many academic works on low-country Georgia, two books stand out. Mart A. Stewart's *"What Nature Suffers to Groe": Life, Labor, and Landscape on the Georgia Coast, 1680–1920* (Athens: University of Georgia Press, 2002) pioneered the environmental history of the southeastern coast. Likewise, Paul M. Pressly's *On the Rim of the Caribbean: Colonial Georgia and the British Atlantic World* (Athens: University of Georgia Press, 2013) puts the same region into a wider, transnational context.

Sandy and Roger, 2015

Several scholars have examined particular layers of Ossabaw Island's rich history in considerable detail and nuance. On early settlement sites, see Charles E. Pearson, "Prehistoric Settlement Sites on Ossabaw Island, Georgia: An Atlas" (Athens: University of Georgia Laboratory of Archaeology Manuscript 614, 2014). Allison Dorsey's chapter "'The great cry of our people is land!': Black Settlement and Community Development on Ossabaw Island, Georgia, 1865–1900," in *African American Life in the Georgia Lowcountry,* ed. Philip Morgan (Athens: University of Georgia Press, 2010) provides a detailed look at the African American experience on Ossabaw in the late nineteenth century. For an excellent, detailed analysis of the Ossabaw Island Project, with valuable oral histories of former participants, see Margaret Ann Keister, "The Ossabaw Island Project, A Program Fostering Creative Production and Experience," (PhD diss., Athens: University of Georgia, 1992).

Chapter 1, which introduces Ossabaw Island, Roger Parker, sensory history, and the island, is a blend of historical and anthropological scholarship. The story of Roger, here as elsewhere, comes from personal interviews conducted between December 2015 and February 2016. Quotes from Sandy West come from Jane Fishman's *The Woman Who Saved an Island*. On the theory of sensory history, two good starting points are Constance Classen, "Foundations for an Anthropology of the Senses," *International Social Science Journal* 49/152 (September 1997): 401–12, and Mark M. Smith, *Sensing the Past: Seeing, Hearing, Smelling, Tasting, and Touching in History* (Berkeley: University of California Press, 2007). On early settlers and the "howling wilderness," see Richard Cullen Rath, *How Early America Sounded* (Ithaca, NY: Cornell University Press, 2004) and Mark M. Smith, *Listening to Nineteenth Century America* (Chapel Hill: University of North Carolina Press, 2001). On my argument that night changes power dynamics, see A. Roger Ekirch, *At Day's Close: Night in Times Past* (New York: W. W. Norton, 2005). The discussion of night also benefited from a paleontology thesis that humans evolved as a prey species. On this argument, see Donna Hart, *Man the Hunted: Primates, Predators, and Human Evolution* (New York: Basic Books, 2005).

Descriptions of the island's cultural and natural resources that begin in chapter 1 and continue throughout were pieced together from multiple sources, including a National Register Nomination form completed by Kenneth H. Thomas, Jr., John R. Morgan, and Richard R. Cloues in 1996. Additional information came from Taylor P. Davis, "Tabby: The Enduring Building Material of Coastal Georgia," (MA thesis, Athens: University of Georgia, 2011); Jane Brown Gillette, "Enchanted Isle," *Historic Preservation* 46/6 (November/December 1995); and conversations with Elizabeth DuBose, executive director of the Ossabaw Island Foundation, and Paul P. Pressly, director of the Ossabaw Island Education Alliance. When information from government documents differed from that of the experts at the Ossabaw Island Foundation, I deferred to the Foundation. On the work of landscape architect Ellen Biddle Shipman, see *Pioneers of American Landscape Design*, eds. Charles A. Birnbaum and Robin Karson (Washington, DC:

National Park Service, 1993) and (no author) *American Landscape Architecture Designers and Places* (Washington, DC: The Preservation Press, 1989).

Chapter 2 opens with quotes by Raymond Williams and Margaret Keister, which can be found in Raymond Williams, *Keywords: A Vocabulary of Culture and Society* (New York: Oxford University Press, 1976) and Margaret Keister, "The Ossabaw Island Project." Although much has been written on the black drink tea, two good starting points are James Kilgo's essay "Place of the Black Drink Tea," in Jack Leigh, James Kilgo, and Alan Campbell, *Ossabaw: Evocations of an Island* (Athens: University of Georgia Press, 2004) and *Black Drink: A Native American Tea*, ed. Charles M. Hudson (Athens: University of Georgia Press, 1979). Information on the island's ecological zones, flora, and fauna come from Georgia Department of Natural Resources, Wildlife Resources Division, "Ossabaw Island Comprehensive Management Plan" (2000) and Mart Stewart's *"What Nature Suffers to Groe."* Passages that reference Henry David Thoreau's *Walden* come from J. Lyndon Shanly, *The Making of Walden with the Text of the First Version* (Chicago: University of Chicago Press, 1957). These passages are juxtaposed with interviews between the author, Jill Stuckey, Roger Parker, and Torrey Kingry. On silence and apocalyptic environmental damage, see Rachel Carson, *Silent Spring* (New York, Mifflin, 1962).

The discussion of Ossabaw's layered environmental, sensory, and social history found in chapter 3 draws considerable inspiration from Stewart's *"What Nature Suffers to Groe"* and Linda King's dissertation "An Eccentric Place of Very High Quality." The discussion on slavery draws from Todd Savitt, *Medicine and Slavery: The Diseases and Health Care of Blacks in Antebellum Virginia* (Urbana: University of Illinois Press, 1978, 2002) and Mark M. Smith, *How Race Is Made: Slavery, Segregation, and the Senses* (Chapel Hill: University of North Carolina Press, 2006). On George Kollock's plantation journals, many of which are digitally available, see George J. Kollock Plantation Journals, 1837–1861, Southern

Tossing apples to "Poco"

"Paul Mitchell"

Historical Collection, University of North Carolina, Chapel Hill. A sizable letter collection of the Kollock family letters appears as a series in the *Georgia Historical Quarterly* between 1949 and 1951. Insight into Reconstruction on Ossabaw Island comes from Dorsey, "'The great cry of our people is land!'" Other chapter sources include the *Georgia Gazette*, Savannah *Daily News Herald,* and E. B. Garriott, "The West Indian Hurricane of September 29–October 2," in *Monthly Weather Review*, ed. Cleveland Abbe, 26/10 (October 1898).

Chapter 4 draws from interviews with Roger Parker, his son Grayling Parker, and his granddaughter Amanda Escher, all conducted in January and February 2016. Demographic information on Roger's upbringing comes from the 1940 US Federal Census and the discussion of "cowboys" in low-country history draws from Walter Edgar's *South Carolina, A History* (Columbia: University of South Carolina Press, 1998). Insight into the daily work on Ossabaw comes from Roger Parker's detailed notebooks, which he kept throughout the 1970s and early '80s. Quotations from Carol Burdick and members of the Ossabaw Island Project come from Margaret Keister's dissertation, "The Ossabaw Island Project."

Putting the preservation of the island into a broader context, the fifth and final chapter draws primarily from *A Richer Heritage: Historic Preservation in the Twenty-First Century*, ed. Robert E. Stipe (Chapel Hill: University of North Carolina Press, 2003); James Cobb, *Georgia Odyssey* (Athens: University of Georgia Press, 2008); Jack Temple Kirby, *Mockingbird Song: Ecological Landscapes of the South* (Chapel Hill: University of North Carolina Press, 2006); and Linda King's dissertation, "An Eccentric Place of Very High Quality." Insight into the relationship between Sandy West and Jimmy Carter comes from interviews with the former president conducted in September 2013 by Mark Finlay and video-taped by Jill Stuckey; Jane Fishman's *The Woman Who Saved an Island*; and the Ossabaw Island and Torrey Family Papers Collection at the Georgia Historical Society in Savannah. For the state's perspective on the purchase of Ossabaw, see the Georgia DNR Commissioner files during Joe Tanner's tenure, contained at the Georgia State Archives. On Carter's environmental record as governor and president, see Peter G. Bourne, *Jimmy Carter: A Comprehensive Biography from Plains to Postpresidency* (New York: Scribner, 1997); and Douglas Brinkley, *The Unfinished Presidency: Jimmy Carter's Journey beyond the White House* (New York: Viking, 1998). On Carter's inaugural address, see James Earl Carter, *Addresses of Jimmy Carter, Governor of Georgia, 1971–1975*, compiled by Frank Daniel (Atlanta: Ben W. Fortson, Jr., Secretary of State, 1975). For more information on Joseph McGill's visit in 2013 to Ossabaw as part of the Slave Dwelling Project, see Tony Horowitz, "Cabin Fever: One Man's Epic Quest to Visit Every Former Slave Dwelling in the United States," *Smithsonian Magazine* 44/6 (October 2013). Insight into the history and ecological destruction caused by hogs in the South comes from Kirby, *Mockingbird Song* and *Wild Pigs of the United States: Their History, Morphology, and Current Status*, eds. John J. Mayer and I. Lehr Brisben, Jr. (Athens: University of Georgia Press, 1981).

The Saltwater Cowboy

Blaze Stuckey

Acknowledgements

IF JILL AND I COULD HAVE PRODUCED A BOOK ENTIRELY through the eyes and ears of Ossabaw's Saltwater Cowboy, we would have eagerly done so. Yet this cowboy began quite wary—at least when he saw me with a tape recorder or pen and paper. It was not that he opposed the idea of starring in a book. Roger just could not give away his story for free. I bribed him. Jill threatened him. Volunteering for free labor such as cutting firewood seemed to work, but this strategy had diminishing returns. To add to our headache, Roger opened up to others with less reservation. At the Ossabaw Island Foundation's annual meeting in January 2016, Roger gave a well-recieved talk about his personal experiences—including details he never shared with us. And when a reporter from the *Atlanta Journal Constitution* showed up asking questions in February, Roger sang like a bird. The silver lining of the reticent cowboy was that it forced us to expand our scope beyond just Roger's experiences to include episodic glimpses into the long history of the island. The result, we believe, is a better product, and we could not be more grateful for Roger's patience and guidance.

While Roger's input was invaluable, this book project never would have occurred without the inspiration—and financial support—of Wayne Johnson. Wayne saw value in a book that exhibited for the first time Jill's photography. His own experience on the island also convinced him that a camera shutter alone cannot capture the full experience, and he predicted that attention to the sensory totality of Ossabaw Island would have wider appeal. What Wayne may not have known when he asked Jill and me to work together is that the project echoed the long history of interdisciplinary projects on Ossabaw Island that Sandy West funded between 1961 and 1983. Wayne's support gave us the ability to see this project to completion.

Along with Wayne's support, many people shared invaluable research and insight into the recent and distant history of Ossabaw Island. Linda Orr King kindly shared her dissertation research and talked me through some of the contemporary history of the island on the phone and in person. Lynn Speno of the Georgia Department of Natural Resources, Historic Preservation Division, helped me track down the National Register nomination from the late 1990s. Later, Elizabeth DuBose and, especially, Paul Pressly were helpful in clarifying discrepancies between the government documentation and current interpretations. Ann Foskey, Abbie Brown, Paula Snyder, Ed Synder, and Amanda Noll read parts or all of the manuscript, and Bob Ellis helped identify birds. The staff at Mercer University Press has been nothing short of remarkable. Any residual errors—inevitable in a project that came together so quickly—are, of course, the fault of the historian alone.

In their own unique ways, Sandy West and President Carter also made this project possible through their lifetime commitment to environmental protection. Their meeting in 1972 began a series of events that led to the protection of such a precious resource for future generations. Simply put, Ossabaw Island would not be what it is today without staunch defenders of nature.

Jill Stuckey and Blaze, headed to Ossabaw

South End Beach